SUCK AN|

HIM RIGHT

HOW TO GIVE GOOD HEAD AND BLOW HIM AWAY WITH HOT BLOWJOB TECHNIQUES

BARRY MORGAN

DEDICATION

To All Women That Desire To Satisfy Their Men
Sexually

.

CONTENTS

CHAPTER 1

INTRODUCTION

Is there any better feeling than pulling off a blow job that you know for a FACT truly rocked your partner's world? Probably not. If you want to give your man back-arching, toe-curling, screaming orgasms that will keep him sexually addicted to you, then you'll find them in this book.

Don't let the name fool you, blowjobs have nothing to do with blowing, though they do involve using your lips, tongue and mouth to make him go wild with pleasure. Whether on its own or as part of the main event, it can be as good as full penetration but can feel even better (for both of you) if you've got the technique down.

A blowjob (or fellatio) is oral sex performed on a man

using the lips, mouth, and tongue to stimulate the penis. Used as part of foreplay or all the way to orgasm.

While blowjobs might seem intimidating, they're easy enough to do when you get the hang of them. It's all about getting in the right position and knowing how to hit the spot. Knowing how to give a good blowjob is a skill worth having, and once you've mastered the blowjob techniques in our guide, it's easy to give him some seriously intense orgasms.The only thing more satisfying than being on the receiving end of great oral sex is knowing that you did a great job performing it on your partner.

Men's favorite pastime (next to sex or possibly the Superbowl) is getting a blow job. Even better, an unsolicited, impromptu he-didn't-even-have-to-ask-for-it kind of job. Some men consider it even more intimate than sex; your warm mouth, tongue, and lips can bring him some of the most thrilling sensations possible.

When a man receives a blowjob, he's generally extremely grateful. If a woman swallows his semen, he looks at it as a huge honor. Don't ask me why because no man could really explain it. If you can learn to truly enjoy the whole process, you'll have an unbelievably happy man on your hands.

The last thing he wants to think is that it's a chore for you. Most often, a woman's resistance to giving one has to do with his hygiene, the taste, or simply not having the confidence of knowing the "right moves" to please him. The good news is that all of these problems can be solved. I promise you can learn to love or at least like giving a blow job.

Going down on your guy can be a hard task... No pun

intended! How do you do it? How do you begin? How do you end? What happens in between? The questions are endless! All we can say is, practice makes both men and women perfect.

If you're worried about how to give a good blow job, then this is the book for you! From how to do it to how to make it last and everything in between, this book will guide you through every bit.

CHAPTER 2

HOW TO INITIATE A BLOWJOB

For a man, there is nothing more pleasurable than an amazing blow job. The problem is that most men complain that women don't really know how to do it. One of the nicest things you as a woman can do is to initiate a blow job without him asking you for one. Here are some of the steps for doing this in a way that will result in great pleasure for him.

Firstly, remember that just by initiating a blow job you will be seen as very special in your man's eyes. Men often feel self conscious about asking for one as they realise that not all women like to give them. Therefore if you as a woman can give him one without waiting to be asked he will be very pleased.

Another very important thing is to show the man that you are enjoying yourself. Making moans of pleasure and doing it enthusiastically will show that you are not just doing it for his sake, but that you are enjoying it too. Knowing that the pleasure is not all one way will allow the man to relax and enjoy it more.

When you initiate a blow job you could start by giving him a look that tells him you want to give him one. Look into his eyes with lust. Put a smile on your face. Look at his penis with pleasure. These are all important gestures, as a man will be looking subconsciously for clues that you might not be wanting to give him oral.

Also, mentally tell yourself that you are going to enjoy the experience. Visualise how much pleasure you will be giving your man. Imagine him moaning and writhing in pleasure. It will start to turn you on and make the experience all the more fun for you too!

Unlike for women, a man doesn't usually take much time to warm up for sex, least of all for oral sex. When you initiate things you can literally go straight for the target, so to speak, without feeling you have to warm him up. In fact the best warmup for a man can often be for you to take his soft penis into your month and to suck him hard.

When you initiate a blow job you can also begin even when he is asleep. It would be a wonderful way for him to wake up in the morning having a beautiful woman (you) sucking on him greedily. This is indeed a great way to initiate a blow job because if he is asleep he won't be able to feel slightly nervous about you giving him oral sex. Try it!

If you are lying in bed and he is awake, start by kissing him on the chest. Lightly stroke his penis with your hand.

7

Then lower your head down his body, gently kissing him along the way. You don't need to linger too long, but it will be a nice bit of warm up for your man. Remember, he doesn't need as much time as you would to prepare to receive oral sex.

If you would like to initiate a blow job but aren't sure how clean he is (and feel it might put you off) you could suggest the two of you have a shower together. You could even start by going down on him in the shower. Kneeling in front of him in the shower will definitely turn him on.

Initiating a blow job without being asked is undoubtedly one of the loveliest ways to please your man. He will love you for it!

CHAPTER 3

GUIDE TO AN AMAZING BLOWJOB

The blow job is the wild west of sex acts. There are no rules, only instincts. For anyone who's ever wondered how to give a blow job, the literal only certainty is that it begins when you put a penis or any phallic item, like a dildo, in your mouth—beyond that, you can suck, lick, kiss, stroke, grind on, sing to, or, yes, even blow on that member if that's what you and your partner are into.

For those who are less experienced in the art of giving head—and believe me, it's way more of an art than a science—it may seem like a great BJ is defined by fancy tongue maneuvers and taking it so deep that you full-on gag on the dick. But the secret to a great blowie is the secret to great sex of any kind: Talk. It. Out.

If you're going down on someone with a penis, you should feel empowered to ask them what they like. Do they usually orgasm from BJs? How do they feel about eye contact, or using your hands? Do they want to be able to hear how much you enjoy having them in your mouth?

It's important to cater to your partner's "seduction style," Is your partner super visual? Are they more tactile? Perhaps they go crazy for certain sounds? Whatever sensations they most respond to, those are certain needs somebody has with regards to the feedback or the connection that they appreciate. And playing to those needs will make all the difference when performing oral sex.

But just as your partner has needs, you should feel similarly empowered to share your own. Maybe you'd rather give head on your back while they kneel over you. May be cum skeeves you out and you'd prefer them to finish somewhere other than your actual pharynx. May be you only like performing oral sex on a peen when said peen is wrapped in a strawberry banana flavored condom. Whatever it is, your needs are just as important as your partner's, and the experience will be way more enjoyable for the both of you if you're happy and comfortable throughout.

You always need to have some sort of enthusiasm when giving head. If you don't want to be there, it's gonna show, so just don't do it. It's important for both parties to know your boundaries.

OK, so you've talked to your partner and learned a bit about their dream BJ. You've established your own BJ parameters. Where do you go from here? For more on how to give a blow job that will blow your partner away, here are all the best tips.

1. Set the mood.

Don't worry, you don't have to bust out some heels and mood lighting every time you give a blow job. But if you feel confident and sexy going into the experience, the overall vibe will just be hotter. To heighten your own enthusiasm, sexologist Goody Howard suggests playing a little background music. "You want to pick a song that makes you feel powerful, beautiful, and desirable," she says. "And then you want to perform oral sex to the rhythm of the song. You can even hum some of the lyrics into the penis. It also helps you keep a rhythm for your breathing, which helps support gag reflex control."

2. Again, ask what they like.

Everyone's different when it comes to sexual preferences, so if you're unsure what to do, simply ask.

What works for one person will not for the other, so getting down to the core is key. You can ask in a sexy way so that it feels like part of the whole event, instead of just asking for directions. Try something like, "I want to suck your dick. How do you want me to do it?" Watch their eyes light up and their penis jump to attention as they give you a play-by-play of exactly what they like.

That being said, if you're not vibing with their suggestions or if whatever they're asking for makes you uncomfortable, you can always say no. You have to be able to express your needs just as well as you can internalize theirs. Also, you never have to give anyone a blow job if it's not your style. Just be straightforward with your partner about your boundaries.

3. Take some of the pressure out of it.

Deciding to give someone a blow job is a certified Big Deal. But that doesn't mean you have to take all the fun out of it. Instead of worrying about giving the perfect blow job, just be in the moment. Laugh if something silly happens. Take breaks for sips of water. Make jokes. Ease the tension with some weird dance moves. Remember, this is about connecting and enjoying—not about putting on a Broadway-worthy performance.

4. Be all kinds of vocal.

Moan, groan, ooh, and ahh. Hell, even throw in a gurgling sound if the mood strikes you. The point is, don't be afraid to make noises or slurpy sounds—it's not only hot, but the vibrations from your mouth will do wondrous things to their peen.

Channel your inner porn star. Exaggerated moaning and sucking and slurping gives an amazing sensation to the penis, and the vibration from slurping adds layers to the pleasure for the receiving partner.

Also, dirty talk is a great way to not only turn up the heat on the situation but give your jaw a rest. Stare into your partner's eyes and say something along the lines of, "you taste so good," "you feel so good in my mouth," "can I suck it harder?" Whether or not you actually do suck it harder doesn't matter, because they'll instantly be closer to coming.

5. Pillows are your friend.

Your comfort is key! Don't be afraid to take breaks. Do you need a neck pillow? Do you need a different position that's going to help you do the job better? "Don't be afraid to say what your needs are in this situation.

Whether you buy a pillow specifically for sex (yes, sex pillows are a thing) or you grab one off of the bed, pillows are one of the most underrated additions to oral. Not only can you put them under your knees if you're giving a kneeling blow job, but you can use them to prop up your partner's hips, which takes some of the neck strain off of you and provides new sensations for them and new positions for you to try.

6. Also, yes, using lube is an A+ move.

Why would you need lube when you have a mouthful of spit? Because spit dries up quick and lube makes everything better. Not only will it keep things slippery, but if you give your mouth a break and use your hand, it'll speed up the process and prevent you from getting lockjaw. Opt for a flavored lube that doesn't taste like a takeout bag and enjoy the fact that you can suck a dick that tastes like strawberries. The joys of modern sex additives!

7. There is no wrong way to give a blow job.

You should just get that out of your head now because, hi, everyone has different tastes, preferences, likes, and wants, which means it's going to vary for every person you're with.

Different people prefer different techniques, and there's no way to know about their favorite unless you ask or listen to their reaction.

8. It's okay to be intimidated.

If you haven't logged much face-to-penis time, the thought of shoving one in your mouth might be a touch overwhelming. That's totally normal. But if you want to experiment with blow jobs and just don't quite know how to begin, Stewart and Howard both recommend getting in some dress rehearsals before hitting the main stage.

"Take a class or three, get familiar," Stewart says. Howard runs an oral sex workshop called "LICK!" in Dallas, Texas, which she says is her "fantastic fellatio workshop that teaches how to add toys to performance and even reach orgasm while giving head." Not in Dallas? Sex educators in most major cities run similar workshops. Give it a Google.

If a workshop isn't your style, Stewart suggests buying a dildo. "The more you're familiar with the type of anatomy—even though it might just be a toy as opposed to a penis—it's important just to have the practice and to be familiar so that you're not going in there totally clueless."

9. Don't just stroke your partner's penis, stroke their ego.

Trust, the mental and emotional build-up to an orgasm is almost as hot as the actual thing. This means that, yes, if you are looking at this blow job as if it's a chore, your partner will know you're not into it. Use this time to focus on catering to your partner. Your endgame is for your partner to feel like their pleasure is the most important thing in the world.

Similarly, oral sex can be a way to communicate admiration between partners. And if it's something that you really love to do, it'll show—and it'll be so appreciated. "It's important that you're savoring the moment and not rushing.

10. Appeal to all of their senses.

Appealing to the five senses (touch, sight, sound, smell, and taste) is a great way to turn on your partner and set the mood. Something as little as burning a nice aromatherapy candle or wearing that perfume your partner loves. Rub their back or squirt some whipped cream in their mouth while you're going at it. Get creative to put their senses in overdrive.

A blow job is not only about the experience itself, but also about the visual aspects, that's sexy for the receiver. What kinds of sounds are you making? Add some sound to show how much you're enjoying the experience. Throw in some dirty talk, or just some dialog and feedback. Check in with other parts of your body—can you rub up against your lover's body as you're giving head? "I think all of those things are important as well.

11. Don't limit the blow job to the penis only.

There are tons of pleasure spots on the body you can stimulate. One I highly, highly recommend you get familiar with is the perineum—the area between your partner's scrotum and anus. It is highly sensitive because it is home to a lot of nerve endings. Giving this area a little attention can intensify pleasure, using your tongue or index and middle fingers to apply pressure there.

12. Dry mouth is a thing, and it's fine to admit it and work around it.

Whether you have dry mouth from nerves, allergy or prescription meds, or even just drinking alcohol prior (which can dehydrate you), dry mouth is quite common and you can find a way to deal with it! A little prep never hurt anyone—keep some chewing gum or sour candies by your bedside to help nudge your salivary glands into production.

You can also prep, like, way beforehand too. If you love giving head but your dry mouth is cramping your style, invest in some Xylitol-based mouthwashes specifically designed for dry mouth like Biotene or Smart Mouth Mouthwash. Xylitol mouthwashes (remember, stay away from alcohol-based as it can cause dryness) actually helps stimulate saliva production and retain better moisture in the mouth.

13. The anecdotal "hack" that going deeper produces more spit might work for some, but you're literally tricking your brain into going into panic mode in order to do it, so don't feel any pressure.

Some people choose to make themselves gag to produce more spit. But if gagging freaks you out, that makes actual physiological sense. The body's response to deep-throating is similar to that of gagging, which is a defense mechanism preventing swallowing or choking."

Basically, when these areas in the back of your throat get triggered in such a way, the stimulation goes from your nerves to your brain's medulla oblongata, which happens to be located near the other areas of the brain that cause you to get teary eyes and produce excess saliva. There's kind of a medical reason it might work, but you're legit like, hitting the "PANIC" button in your brain to get there. So you can weigh the pros and cons.

14. Not everyone can orgasm from a blow job.

Not everyone will orgasm from a blow job, and that's totally fine. While movies, books and TV shows might make it seem like blow jobs are the holy grail and The Ultimate Thing that all penis-owners want 24/7, some people aren't crazy about them, and others like them (or even love them) but they just don't lead to orgasms.

If you're going at it for ages and nothing's happening, and your partner's like, "Yeah, I might not finish from this since I rarely can," do not take it personally. Trust that they know their body better than you can and try to just enjoy the moment without being so goal-oriented.

15. You don't have to do the kneeling-in-front position if you don't want to.

There's a time and place for kneeling blow jobs and there's also a time and place to be like, "Fuck it, I want to be comfortable and keep movement from where I am right now to a minimum." If you try changing up your position so you sit next to them, not in front of them, you can change the sensation for your partner, show off your ass, and you might find that it just makes things comfier for you on the whole.

16. Go ahead and make it about you too!

Bringing a vibrating toy into things can make giving head even hotter. You can use one hand to hold it while you're kneeling and sort of sit on it for maximum control.

To cum while you're going to town on your partner, lying on your back with your partner on their knees is suggested. Turn to the right to give them a blowjob while they finger you. For extra pleasure, use a vibrating toy on yourself. Watching one another experience the shared pleasure can be a massive turn-on for both you and your partner.

17. Your partner might be quiet but still be absolutely lovin' it.

This is a problem among people with penises, many of whom seem to have been told, at some point, to literally never exude enthusiasm in sex. If your partner's silence is weirding you out, tell them so! Positive feedback is helpful for BJ novices and experts alike.

18. You can also do this in the shower.

Most shower sex is difficult to impossible—the literal black diamond of sex locations. But oral sex is both doable and enjoyable in the shower. Have your partner stand out of the jet stream (so you can be in it) and go to town after you've watched them wash their body.

19. Balls exist and maybe you should incorporate them into this whole thing.

But don't do it without first asking if your partner is into that. And then follow that question up with, "And how do you like your balls played with?" Because what people who don't have them don't know is that apparently, they're very sensitive! So don't go yanking away without warning.

If you have strong abs, kneel between [your partner's]

legs and use one hand on the shaft and the other to gently pull and caress the balls.

20. Also, this is a good time to address the butt.

Once again: Ask your partner if they like butt play before you venture into unknown territory. And then if they give you the all-clear, ask again what kind of play they like. This also tends to speed up blow jobs, which, you know, might be a good thing.

21. Not to be a bummer, but you can get STIs from this.

Which is why wearing condoms during oral is a good idea, especially for new, non-monogamous partners. There are plenty of flavored varieties if the taste of latex isn't really your thing.

22. Get creative and be playful.

Bring some toys (vibrators feel good on penises, too!) into the mix, or try some flavored lubes. Take a play from Samantha Jones's book and have them stand in front of a mirror. It can be super hot to watch yourself get it on. Use that over-the-door mirror you've had since freshman year of college for dirty purposes and position yourselves in front of it while you go down on your partner.

Hungry? Howard suggests adding some fruit roll ups (yes, you read that right) into your sexy repertoire. Instead of using the whole thing all at once, which could take a while to work your way through, cut that fruity goodness into three sections and wrap one of them

around the middle of the shaft. This will give you an incentive to get more penis in your mouth and you won't be sucking dick for like, a whole week.

23. You can speed up the process by adding foreplay.

For some people, blow jobs are foreplay that leads up to other stuff. For others, they're the main event. Whatever the case may be, you can blow their freakin' mind and detract minutes from the amount of time their D is in your M by teasing your partner pre–blow job. Get them all worked up by kissing their hips and thighs, then their shaft. Breathe on the tip of their dick, lick it lightly. Flirt with it! Not only does it feel great for them, but it's fun for you and it can cut down on the amount of time you're actually sucking and straining your jaw.

24. They're paying less attention to what your face looks like than you think they are.

Have you ever seen anyone eat a really big popsicle? Like, put their whole dang mouth around it (which, ouch, brain freeze)? It's not a dainty sight! And that's okay.

When you're giving a blow job, you're not supposed to look super composed and photo-ready. Your mouth is on your lover's genitals. They're gonna think you look hot no matter what.

25. It isn't a fancy massage at a spa, and therefore, doesn't have to be all about them.

Ever heard of something called sensate focus? It's a sex therapy technique in which you focus on touch and the physical pleasure it brings you, and you can totally use it to ease blow job anxiety or just ~mix it up~ a little. Basically, instead of doing what you think you're supposed to do to make them feel great, employ blow job techniques that feel fun and exciting to you. Oral sex doesn't have to be as one-sided as its reputation would imply.

26. A penis isn't a vagina or a Slip'N Slide and

doesn't just get wet on its own.

I mean, there's pre-ejaculate, but that's like a light rain shower when a proper BJ usually requires a torrential downpour. Drink some water and be prepared to use all the spit you can muster. Don't be afraid to literally spit on their penis if things get dry. It's not gross. This is someone you make out with (probably), and trust me, they'll think it's hot.

27. You do not have to bow down before their erect penis like it's royalty.

In movies and TV shows, the only BJ position ever depicted is someone on their knees, bobbing their head back and forth while their partner stands up like a statuesque Greek god. You don't have to invest in knee pads like Stephanie from seventh grade said you would! Stephanie lied to you. Just get on the bed and do it lying down. It's comfier!

28. You don't have to swallow their semen, but you can if you like it.

No shade to the folks who like the taste and feel of cum in their mouth, but for some people, the sensation is icky. That doesn't mean your partner's not a total babe and you aren't mega attracted to them—it just means the two of you should figure out an alternative cum route. Maybe they orgasm on your chest? How about into a tissue or towel? Chat about it with your lover to find a solution that you both think is delicious and sexy.

29. Your hands can pinch-hit when your mouth needs some time on the bench.

Your hands are an incredible BJ asset that can be used at the same time as your mouth, and also in moments when your mouth needs a break. Use your hands and stroke the penis while performing oral sex especially when they get ready to cum. You can stroke the penis and angle it away from your mouth and take that time to focus on the testicles. Using tools like a hand job sleeve can make it easier for someone with hand issues or arthritis.

30. You're not going to accidentally bite down on the penis with your teeth and sever it and leave your partner sterile forever.

There are an inordinate number of horror stories about people who accidentally use their teeth during a BJ and skin their partner's dick with their razor molars or something. This is not—I repeat, not—a regular occurence. Have some awareness of where your teeth are in relation to their penis so that you avoid causing them any pain or discomfort, but don't let it get to your head (or either one of theirs).

31. Sometimes a penis doesn't smell good, and that's okay.

I don't think anyone expects a hard penis to smell like Chanel perfume or a strawberry Lip Smacker, but some people have a stronger scent than others. Anyone's crotch area can get sweaty and pungent. If you're concerned about your partner's smell or hygiene, kindly suggest a sexy shower together before any mouth-to-genital action.

32. Your tongue is your BJ BFF.

It's not the strongest muscle in your body for no reason, okay?! Tongues are sexy as hell, and the chances are high that your partner's going to want to see yours in action as you lick the living daylights outta their phallus. While giving head, play around with tongue shapes: Wide and flat on the shaft and tight and pointy on the tip are two good places to start. Licking their shaft while holding eye contact, and tickling your tongue across the shaft as you go up and down is damn sexy.

Also, you can use your tongue to trick them into thinking they're all the way in your mouth, like magic, if magic were sexier. Just either tuck their penis underneath your tongue or use your tongue to block the back of your throat (this also protects your delicate gag reflexes just in case).

33. A blow job isn't like a magic button that makes someone cum right now immediately.

Although people do seem to love them, it's not something that begins and ends in a matter of seconds (usually). These things can be a lot of work, especially if you're down there for like 15 minutes. You can quit whenever you want though—never feel like you're dropping out of a race early.

34. Porn can actually teach you a lot about blow jobs, like the graphic sex education you never had in school.

Sex education should definitely be better in this country, but I really doubt we'll ever have gym coaches teaching good blow job decorum in front of a bunch of confused teenagers. And that's probably for the best? Anyway. People don't tend to fuck like they do in porn, but sometimes those close-up shots of someone ferociously sucking a D can serve as good little tutorials on how to move your head. Just don't attempt deep-throating if you're not very experienced.

Once you've gotten your porny techniques down, Hirschman recommends trying to create some suction, kind of like a vacuum, right when you feel the tip of their dick get the hardest. This creates an extremely powerful orgasm.

35. Literally no one can deep-throat without gagging.

I vaguely remember some girl in ninth grade telling me that all grown women literally swallow lidocaine or the stuff in those Orajel swabs before giving a blow job so they don't gag on a dick. Don't do this! Don't drink lidocaine! No! If you're worried about gagging or throwing up on someone you like, the solution is to just not deep-throat a penis.

36. You do not have to give a BJ just to get head in return.

If someone refuses to go down on you because you don't like giving BJs, or for literally any other reason, they suck (except they don't suck, hahaha get it?). This is the epitome of thank you, next. There are tons of people out there who are going to love the idea of going down on you, so go find them!

37. Enjoying giving and/or receiving oral sex isn't an indicator of how good you are in bed, okay?

In fact, it says nothing about you other than that you enjoy and/or don't enjoy giving and/or receiving oral sex. This one sex act is way overblown (had to, sorry), but it's just one thing on an endless menu of sexy stuff you can do with another person. Blow jobs can be super hot and build lots of juicy intimacy, but they're not the end-all-be-all if you don't want them to be. Trust your gut (and your gag reflex) and you can't go wrong.

CHAPTER 4

BLOWJOB TECHNIQUES

Knowing the best blowjob techniques to bring your man into a state of orgasmic bliss is vital if you want to make him utterly addicted to you...or any man for that matter.

That's what this chapter of the Blow Job Guide is all about, teaching you most powerful blow job techniques. You have finished reading this general tips and guidelines on how to give head in the previous chapter. Now let's learn some blow job techniques to make your man's eyes roll into the back of his head, and his toes curl in pleasure.

1. Lick, Lick, Lick It

Licking his penis is a powerful blow job technique for beginning your blow job. It serves as a sort of oral sex foreplay that will build sexual tension and have him begging you to take him in your mouth...which is exactly what you want.

Licking his cock is super easy. At it's simplest, you just need to hold his penis in your hands and use your tongue to lick it. You'll find that licking him from the base to the tip works really well. But don't stop here, there are a bunch of other licking techniques that you can use during your blow job:

• **Focus on the Tip**

According to one study, the top part or glans of your man's penis is the most sensitive part, specifically the underside of his glans. But if your man is circumcised, then it will be slightly less sensitive. The bottom side, where the head connects to his shaft, is known as the frenulum and is also incredibly sensitive. Although, some studies find that the whole glans is sensitive with no one part more sensitive than the other.

Try focusing on licking the tip of his penis (the glans) using the least amount of pressure possible. Many guys report this being their absolute favorite blow job technique. You can even try doing this for your entire blow job until he comes.

• The Topside of your Tongue

The top side of your tongue provides slightly more stimulation than the underside thanks to the rough surface your taste buds create. So focus on using the top side of your tongue when licking him.

• His Balls

Don't forget about his balls. His balls are as sensitive as his penis, and for some guys, even more sensitive. You can simply lick them.

•Anilingus

There are two other excellent locations besides his penis and balls that can massively add to his pleasure and make him see you as an oral sex goddess even if they are not strictly part of a regular BJ.

His perineum or perineal raphe aka his taint, the rough patch of skin located just behind his balls as well as his anus contain a lot of nerve endings. The root of his penis lies beneath this skin, behind the perineum, so you can stimulate it through his perineum. Some guys adore having these two areas licked and stimulated while others don't like it at all. It's a personal preference, and it all depends on your man.

Tonguing these areas, up and down, or in a circular

motion is an awesome way to stimulate them. You can even press your tongue inwards on his anus to provide a different, but still pleasurable sensation. This technique is called anilingus.

• **Taint-To-Tip**

A technique that works great if your man has a sensitive perineum (taint) or balls is to slowly lick him from his perineum all the way to the tip of his penis. Doing this in one slow, continuous lick is best.

You'll also find that it's easiest to do when you use your hand or just a finger to press his penis against his belly.

One vital blow job technique to keep in mind when licking his dick during a blow job is that:

➤ **Wetter Is Better**

Ask any guy, and they will tell you the same thing: Super

wet blow jobs feel best. Ideally, you will easily be able to produce lots of saliva on command, but that's not always easy.

Two tricks to producing more saliva are:

• Chewing gum right before going down on him.

• Eating a piece of juicy fruit before you start blowing him (like a strawberry or pineapple or peach).

Of course, these two tricks aren't always practical.

A much easier and more reliable way to make your blow jobs super-wet is to use edible lube. Just keep some handy in a drawer beside your bed or in your purse. This also means that you will have lube handy in case you need some for sex.

➢ **Deep Throating Solution**

One quick way to produce lots of saliva is to deep throat

your man. Here's why it works:

When his penis touches the back of your throat, it will stimulate your gag reflex. This triggers your body to quickly produce lots of saliva. So, if you both enjoy deep throat, this is the perfect technique to give your man a wet, sloppy blow job.

2. Just The Tip

As I mentioned earlier, the tip of your man's penis (the glans) is by far the most sensitive spot on his penis, particularly the underside. The female equivalent of the penis is the clitoris. So focusing your attention on the tip of his penis is going to work well to push him over the edge in the most intense and pleasurable way possible.

There are a number of different techniques you can use to pleasure the tip of his penis.

• Kissing

Kissing the tip of his penis is a fabulous technique to start off your blow job and draw out the length of it...perfect if you like seeing and hearing your man squirm in beautiful agony. Kissing his penis and balls is easy, just think back to how you kiss him normally (on the lips)...

• Purse your lips together and give him small "pecks."

• Open your lips slightly so that you can gently squeeze the tip of his penis between them.

• With saliva on your lips, gently run them over his penis.

• Use your lips to gently suck on the top of his penis.

• The Twister

Using your tongue and lots of saliva, you can perform an ultra-pleasurable and satisfying blow job technique I like to call the Twister. While holding his penis steady in one or both hands, start making a slow circular motion with your tongue around the top of his penis. You can alternate direction and speed to add some variety, but this blissful bj technique alone is enough to bring him to a thundering climax.

• Deep Throat

Deep throating your man is a more advanced blow job technique, but when done right, it can deeply gratify and sexually satisfy your man. This extra pleasure is thanks to the back of your throat. As you take him deep into your mouth, eventually, your tonsils and the back of your throat will come into contact with the tip of his penis.

The slight spasming of your throat (thanks to your gag reflex) will make it more enjoyable and stimulating for your man, along with the fact that the rest of your mouth and tongue will be stimulating the shaft of his dick.

• The Tip Of The Tip

Some guys have sensitive urethral openings. That's the small slit at the very top of his penis where his cum comes out of. Try gently licking it when giving him a blow job and judge his reaction. If he enjoys it, then he's one of those guys who enjoys it. If he doesn't, then just move on to another technique.

• Slip Inside

A less advanced fellatio technique that is almost as effective at providing him with intense delight and stimulation as deep throating him is using the inside of your mouth. By taking him into your mouth and pressing/rubbing the tip of his penis against the inside of your cheek and tongue, you have another tool for your blow job arsenal.

• Use The Roof

Carrying on from the previous technique, there's another option for stimulating him: the roof of your mouth. While you might not think it can help you when giving him a blow job, you'd be wrong.

The texture feels great when you angle his penis so that the top of his glans moves against the ridges on the roof of your mouth. If the size of his penis and your mouth don't allow you to change angles or would mean he gets scraped with teeth, then you should probably avoid this technique.

• Fingers & Hands

Using your fingers and hands is not strictly a blow job technique. However, using them is a great way to give your mouth and jaw a break. With plenty of saliva or lube, try gently running your fingers over and back the top of his penis and listen as he uncontrollably groans in pleasure.

3. The Up & Down

Almost all guys fantasize about getting a blow job, but if you're not feeling particularly confident the first few times you try it, then my advice is to stick to the easy-to-perform blow job techniques like the Up & Down.

Mastering this first is a smart way to get comfortable giving your boyfriend a blow job before progressing to more advanced techniques and tactics for giving him oral pleasure like sucking him.

To perform the Up & Down, you simply need to take your man's penis into your mouth and make a tight "O" shape with your mouth around his penis. This "O" shape means that you can apply pressure around his entire penis.

Next, you are simply going to bob your head up and down, taking his penis in and out of your mouth. Bobbing your head up and down is super simple to start with, especially if you just concentrate on the top inch or two of his penis. As you get comfortable with this, try taking him deeper and deeper with each stroke so that you can stimulate more and more of his penis.

Taking him deeper and deeper into your mouth runs the risk of triggering your gag reflex. Try not to worry about this. It's entirely natural, and most men don't really care if you gag a little.

Note: There is a ridge on his penis, where his head joins the shaft. This ridge is particularly sensitive for your man when stimulated. Try focusing on it with your lips when you make the "O" shape.

Focusing on this part of his penis also means that you are only taking the first 1-2 inches of his penis into your mouth, making gagging less likely. If you feel yourself getting close to gagging, it's okay to pause, breathe, and relax your throat.

4. Tongue Tricks

There are two other blow job techniques that involve your tongue. One is easy to perform, while the other is slightly more tricky but wildly satisfying for your man.

• Soft Sandpaper

Don't let the name fool you. This will NOT feel like sandpaper for your man; it will feel fantastic. The reason I call it "Soft Sandpaper" is because you will be using your tastebuds to "polish" your man's penis in a similar motion that you would use with sandpaper. But the similarities end there.

To start, hold the shaft of your man's penis firmly in your hand, then make your tongue as wet as possible and stick it out.

Next...

While holding your head and tongue in place, use your hand to move the head of his penis over your tongue. So, the only movement should be from your hand moving his penis over your tongue. Your tongue shouldn't be moving much at all. This way, the head of his penis will be running over your tongue.

You can move it in a circular motion, up & down, back and forth, or any movement you like. In this way, your tongue is "polishing" the head of his penis.

• Sliding Shaft

For this technique, take his penis as deep into your mouth as you find comfortable and hold it there. 2, 4, or 6 inches deep are all fine. The key is making sure you find it easy and comfortable to hold it there.

Next...

With your tongue at the underside of his penis, you need to slide it forwards along his shaft, as far as you can comfortably go and then slide it backward. Keep sliding it forward and backward, massaging the same section of his shaft.

While you are doing this, keep his penis in place. Don't take it deeper or shallower; just keep it in place.

Sliding Shaft is not a breakthrough blow job technique that is going to make your man immediately explode, but it's a great little trick to use if you want to change your blow job routine and add some new sensations for your man.

5. BJ Techniques When He's Uncut

Most of the blow job techniques listed above work best when your man is circumcised or "cut." While some of the tips transfer without any adjustments if your man is uncircumcised or "uncut," others need adjustments, and some BJ techniques won't work at all.

There's no need to worry, however! There are some special techniques that you can only use on guys that are uncircumcised. The difference is that uncut guys have extra foreskin, also known as the prepuce, which partially or completely covers the glans. Uncut guys also have more frenulum along the underside of their glans.

• Pull it back

The foreskin gets tighter when a man is erect, but the tightness varies, so you'll need to get used to his foreskin when blowing him. Some foreskin is pretty tight when the guy is hard, so there's not much wiggle room there.

But not too much – This might seem confusing, but pulling the foreskin all the way back can be quite uncomfortable for some guys. So you don't need to push it as far back as it can go, just enough to expose at least part of the head. A guy won't feel much if you're stimulating him through his foreskin, so you need to pull it back to have direct access to the head of his penis.

Switch it up – Pulling back the foreskin means you can focus on just the tip of his penis using the techniques from above, but this can become overwhelming for a guy who is uncut. According to research, cut guys are less likely to ask their partner to be gentler on their penis, they want more stimulation; although, women may not always notice a difference in sensitivity. Remember that the foreskin causes an uncut guy's glans to be extra sensitive, so you may want to let the foreskin move back into place from time to time.

Use the foreskin – You can actually stroke the foreskin across his glans, which feels great for many uncut guys. You can also use this time to give your mouth a break! It's also a good way to give him less stimulation and make your blow job last longer.

Swirl your tongue – When you're ready to take his penis back into your mouth, keep the foreskin down over his penis and insert your tongue between the head of his cock and foreskin. Give it a swirl or three. He's sure to enjoy it! Roll your tongue around as you push the foreskin back off his glans.

Suck and squeeze, gently – If a guy is uncut, you can orally stimulate his foreskin as well as the glans and shaft. This is a technique for a good blow job that will set you apart from other women who may not be sure how to go down on an uncut cock. Suckle and squeeze your lips around his foreskin. Start gently and SLOWLY increase the intensity.

Remember that each guy has his own preference for how much pressure and foreskin attention he likes, which is why it's essential for you to talk to him about what he likes.

6. Anal Action

Your man's ass contains a lot of nerve endings, thousands in fact, and it's begging for some stimulation.

This means that there is no better time to introduce anal play than during your blow job. It can literally triple the pleasure you give him.

Here are a few ways to add anal play to your oral sex.

Rubbing his perineum – I've already talked about stimulating your man's perineum during your blow job. It's pretty straightforward, you can run your fingers over it, teasing it, or you can press it gently/firmly depending on how much pressure he enjoys. Some prostate toys have an external arm to stimulate his taint easily.

Teasing his asshole – Try gently running your fingers over his asshole or even making small circles over it. This is a great way to gauge his reaction and see if he enjoys it. Just like you, he may adore anal play during oral sex, hate it, or be indifferent to it.

If he enjoys it, then you'll want to continue. Remember, you can use a bit of lube/saliva to make it slicker.

Fingering him – Taking it to the next level, you can start penetrating him with your finger, pressing it in and out.

Prostate Pleasure – A further step during your blow job, is penetrating him about 2 inches deep with your finger and stimulating his prostate (aka the male G Spot). Keeping your fingertips and palm against his perineum, slide one finger into his ass and curl it back towards his penis when you are 2 inches deep.

You should feel a soft fleshy nub. This is his prostate, and you can stimulate it just like you stimulate your own G Spot by gently pressing it and rubbing it.

You can even use a toy to stimulate his prostate while you focus on his dick with your mouth.

Pulling out during orgasm – When you keep your finger inside as he cums, you'll notice that his ass rhythmically pulsates during his climax. This "clenching" sensation around your fingers with his ass during orgasm can be pleasurable for him, but other guys prefer something else…. When you slowly pull your finger out as he orgasms.

The best way to find out what he prefers: you keeping your finger in his ass during orgasm or slowly pulling it out is to ask him — however, the fun way is to try both and judge for yourself what he likes most.

Lube and nails – Lastly, make sure to use lube when penetrating him anally and also trim/file your nails so that you don't accidentally cut or hurt him. Lube is also essential for anal penetration since the anus doesn't self-lubricate like the vagina.

7. Triple Trick

My most powerful blow job technique is called the Triple Trick technique.

It's not particularly challenging to perform, but it does require a bit of coordination. Here's how to do it:

Part 1 – Take the head of your man's penis into your mouth and start performing the Twister on it (I cover this technique above).

Part 2 – At the same time, take one hand, wrap it around his shaft and start to jerk him off while performing the Twister.

Part 3 – Insert a lubed finger into his ass and start to massage his prostate.

You'll be performing all three blow job techniques at the same time, which requires a good degree of coordination, as I mentioned before. And that's all there is to delivering triple the pleasure to your man.

8. Enjoying Yourself & Putting On A Show

You know that fulfilling feeling of seeing your man in deep pleasure, close to orgasm, and unable to control himself? It's incredibly hot.

Well, here's a secret about most men...

• They feel the exact same way about you.

• They get off to seeing you enjoy yourself.

Keep this in mind the next time you go down on your man. If you are already naturally enjoying yourself as you give him a blow job, awesome! Of course, there are other ways to further enjoy yourself during your blow job.

Try masturbating and bringing yourself to orgasm as you

blow him. This serves multiple purposes:

• It put's on a show for your man (most men get visually turned on).

• You show your man how much you are enjoying yourself, giving him a blow job, which is a pretty great way to satisfy his ego.

• You get to orgasm too!

9. Suck On Penis

A powerful, but often tiring technique is sucking your man's penis. Of course, you're not doing this to "suck" the come out of him, that would be impossible! Instead, you're going to wrap your lips around his penis and take the first few inches of it into your mouth.

Then you are going to suck on it gently. Sucking on it will cause your lips and the inside of your mouth to press softly against his shaft and the head of his cock, stimulating the length of it. While doing this, you can take his penis in and out of your mouth, allowing you to pleasure it entirely.

While sucking him, you can add some variation by using your tongue to massage his penis too. There isn't anything more to this technique other than simply sucking and taking his penis in and out of your mouth.

10.69ing Your Man

I'm only going to talk briefly about 69ing your man, as I already have an entire guide about 69ing.

As you probably already know, using the 69 position is a great blow job technique to share the pleasure with your man and reach simultaneous orgasm.

But the most important thing you should know about

69ing your man is that… The BEST 69 position is for him to lie on his back with you on top of him. This way, you control how deep you take him.

The problem when he's on top, is that he's the one in control…which isn't great if you gag easily.

Using the same techniques over and over can eventually become boring for your man (and you!), so it's best to have a few tricks up your sleeve to change things up at a moment's notice.

Some women think that to vary things; they need an endless list of blow job techniques and different things they can do with their mouth or tongue or lips to provide different sensations to their man. The truth is, you don't. There are much simpler ways to spice up your blow job routine.

One way is by adding what I like to call "Awesome Sauce" to your blow jobs. Awesome Sauce is just using something like maple syrup, chocolate syrup, cream, champagne, ice cream, or even ice cubes in your mouth while you go about your regular blow job routine. Here are a few tips on using each.

Maple Syrup/Chocolate Syrup/Cream – All of these tasty treats work super well because they taste great, AND they provide a different but very enjoyable sensation to your husband as you fellate him. Just make sure that if you are using warm chocolate syrup that it's not so hot that it burns him!

Ice Cubes/Ice Cream – Cold sensations are not the most popular type of Awesome Sauce during oral sex, but they still work well for switching things up and keeping your man on his toes.

Champagne – There is something intensely sexy about champagne, especially when you use it during a BJ. The next time you and your man have some alone time, try slipping into some lingerie and popping open a bottle of champagne. Next, have a little sip and with the champagne in your mouth, take your man in your mouth and start performing fellatio on him.

The bubbles provide your man with new and different sensations, but it's not just that. There is something about the entire act of giving your man a champagne blow job and making him cum that is super arousing and sexy. Don't like champagne? A fizzy soda can do the trick.

Mints – Mint naturally creates a cooling sensation. If you suck one before going down, you don't have to juggle the mint and his penis in your mouth at the same time.

The added benefit of having champagne or ice cream or

anything tasty in your mouth is that it drowns out the taste of his sperm and semen when he does ejaculate. Perfect if you can't stand how he tastes.

Pro tip: To prevent the champagne flowing out of your mouth, make sure you are below your man when giving him head, so being on your knees while he is standing works well here.

11. Give Him A Hand

Using your hands is a powerful blow job technique while giving your man oral sex. And in case you're wondering, it's NOT cheating! In fact, you can give your guy way more pleasure and enjoyment by using your hands on his penis and balls during your blow job. While the in-depth Hand Job Guide will teach you the most pleasurable hand job techniques you need to know, here's three that you can start using tonight.

Jerk & Suck – Jerking your man off while giving him a handjob at the same time is a super way to maximize his pleasure. Simply take the first inch or two of his penis into your mouth and then wrap one hand around his shaft. While using a simple technique like the Suck On This technique I described earlier, you can also run your hand up and down his shaft at the same time, giving him a handjob.

Time To Rest – If you aren't used to blowing your man, then you will naturally find that your jaw and mouth get tired quite quickly. Allowing your hands to take over while you give your mouth a rest means that your man gets to receive unbroken pleasure.

So when you feel your mouth becoming tired, grab hold of his penis and start jerking him off for a minute or two. Then when your mouth is rested, you can go back to giving him oral sex.

Work His Balls – Another great hand job technique you can incorporate into your blow job is working his testicles or balls. There are so many different things that you can do to his testicles with your hands while giving him a blow job, from fondling to caressing to tickling to massaging them. Try experimenting to see what your man enjoys the most. The testicle massage guide will give you more ideas.

12. Play Ball(s)

Speaking of working your man's testicles...using your mouth to stimulate them is an excellent blow job technique that adds even more pleasure to his experience. Whatever you can do to his penis with your mouth, you can do to his balls. The only significant difference is that your man's testicles are super sensitive to pain, so make sure you don't apply too much pressure...or worse accidentally use your teeth on him!

Kiss His Balls – An easy way to see if your man enjoys you playing with his balls is to start by gently kissing them. Just purse your lips together and give them a few soft, wet kisses.

Lick His Balls – Once you can see how much he enjoys you kissing his balls, take it up a notch by gently licking and massaging them with your tongue. Keeping your tongue flat so that it covers as much of his testicles as possible is best.

Suck His Balls – A more intense way to massage his balls with your mouth is to gently take them into your mouth and softly massage them with your tongue. Remember, the keyword here is SOFTLY. You'll also find that the more saliva you use, the silkier it feels for your man. Edible lubricant works great here too.

So you can kiss them, lick them and even suck them. A powerful technique is gently taking one of his balls into your mouth and then softly licking and sucking on it.

Remember that different guys have different preferences. So while some guys adore having their balls stimulated, a small percentage of guys don't enjoy it much at all. Don't worry about this as it's just your man's personal preference. If your husband or boyfriend does enjoy it, then you'll find that it's much easier for you to pleasure his balls if he trims his hair down there.

13. Use Toys

Don't be afraid to use sex toys during your blow job! There are so many things you can do with them.

• Rub your vibrator up and down his penis, balls or ass as

you suck him off.

• Put a cock ring on your man. Find out how to use a cock ring.

• Get your man to wear a but plug or prostate massager during your blow job. More info on butt plugs.

• Use your vibrator on yourself during your blow job and put on a show for your man. Learn how to use a vibrator.

• Tie his hands behind his back with your handcuffs/bondage gear. Get tips for tying him up safely.

These ideas are just scratching the surface on how to use sex toys during your blow job. If you have any of your own ideas, please feel free to share them in the comments section below.

14. Eye To Eye: All About Eye Contact

Making eye contact with your man while giving him

head can be super intimate and intense and even a bit submissive.

The key to doing it right is understanding two caveats…

Too Intense? – If you have just started dating your man and you proceed to give him a ten-minute blow job maintaining unbroken, unblinking eye contact throughout, then he is obviously going to feel a little uncomfortable. It's going to feel too intense.

To prevent this, just tone down the amount of eye contact you are making or just look at him for 2-3 seconds at a time

Don't Force It – Similar to ensuring you don't make overly intense eye contact, is making sure that you don't force it either. You can immediately break the sexual tension and kill the atmosphere if you are trying awkwardly to maintain eye contact with your man during a blow job.

So if you notice that your boyfriend always breaks eye contact with you or gets uncomfortable whenever you try to make eye contact with him during oral sex (or even during regular sex for that matter), then just forget about using this technique and try something else.

15. For Quick Comers/Cummers

If your man cums easily and quickly, then there are two simple techniques you can use to prolong his blowjob and pleasure.

1. Focus on the methods that don't make him lose control and cum – This may seem obvious, but many women often forget about this. As I mentioned above, the tip of your man's penis is the most sensitive, so avoid stimulating the tip if you want him to last longer. Instead, focus on his shaft, balls, perineum, and ass along with the techniques that don't quickly bring him to the edge.

2. Light as a feather – Use a minimum amount of pressure when stimulating him if you don't want him to cum quickly. So, when you take his penis into your mouth, he should barely feel it.

3. Take a break – Take a moment to caress his body with your hands, kiss up his tummy to suck on his nipples, or even kiss your man if he doesn't want to come just yet.

Two Steps Forward And One Step Backward

You know that beautiful agony you feel as you build up to cumming at a snail's pace, and then your man backs off a bit...then he again starts building you up even closer to orgasm? You wish it would come faster, but the entire slow, drawn-out process is still incredibly enjoyable. More importantly, all that build-up makes your orgasm feel far more intense when you do eventually climax. Well...why not use this to your advantage.

The next time you are giving your man a blow job, try backing off a bit and spend a minute or two doing something else entirely like:

• Giving him a handjob.

• Fondling his ball.

• Performing anilingus.

• Just kissing him.

Then after a few minutes, return to giving him a blow job. This variation is great for spicing up your regular routine…but it also has the effect of intensifying his orgasm when he eventually peaks and climaxes. Keep in mind that for some guys, if you keep him aroused for a long time without orgasm, he will get blue balls where his balls actually start hurting.

CHAPTER 5

BLOWJOB MISTAKES TO AVOID

If your guy is getting regular oral sex, he certainly isn't going to complain. And if he's getting off, you're obviously doing something right (Though that's the beauty of a blowjob; it's good when it's good and it's good when it's bad).

But wouldn't it be great to know if you're really doing it right? There are tried-and-true techniques for oral sex and there are some more creative options to make your partner squeal, but those sexy tricks mean nothing if you're making a mistake with his precious penis.

Do you know what to avoid? Though there are obvious no-nos (like going sans lube or, you know, breaking his penis bone), you may be making some mistakes without knowing you're suppressing his orgasm.

Keep reading for some common mistakes—plus simple fixes—to your oral sex conundrums.

1. Keeping your hands to yourself

The major mistake women make in the oral sex department is thinking a hand job and blowjob are two totally separate things. In reality, a BJ is just a hand job with a bonus.

While using your mouth is a key part of the oral equation, do not forget to put your hands to work! They can stroke his shaft, tug on his balls or even give him a sexy show by touching yourself.

If you're open to it, some guys even like a little tickle around the booty, and you'd probably rather use your fingers than your tongue for that one.

2. Not Using Your Tongue

If you are just going up and down like a vacuum, you're doing it wrong. Just as kissing without your tongue is extremely boring and oddly chaste, so is keeping your tongue in one spot for the entire duration of a blow job. Ideally, as your mouth goes up and down his shaft, your tongue should be doing the same thing. But I don't mean like, you should just rest your tongue there while your mouth moves—you need to move it around.

3. Ignoring The Balls

Not surprising that a common hand job mistake is often a blow job mistake too. Look, I know that balls are weird and, minus the whole "making testosterone and sperm" thing, seem kind of pointless. Like they're just... there? But actually no, you shouldn't treat the balls like that annoying coworker who says "Happy Humpday" and act like they don't exist. If you really want to go from giving the blow job equivalent of cold pizza to serving up kobe beef BJs (IDK, just go with me on the food analogy here), you're going to need to touch the balls. Play with them with your hands (gently), put them in your mouth (one at a time so you don't choke), just do something.

4. Focusing on the head

The head of the penis is always donned as his super sensitive area, but it isn't his most sensitive! For a circumcised guy, the area of his circumcision scar is filled with nerve endings. If he isn't circumcised, he'll feel insane pleasure pretty much anywhere; when a guy gets snipped, it deadens five super sensitive pleasure zones on his penis!

He also feels some strong sensations on the perineum— the spot between his anus and scrotum—that your hands or tongue can play with while you work.

5. That gross gagging sound

If you learn most of your sexual repertoire from porn—
and face it, you probably do—let's get one thing straight.
Deep throat really isn't that great. And if your guy thinks
it is, it's because porn has conditioned him to think that
he should.

If you have the gag reflex of a normal person, deep throat
will cause you to make that gross gagging noise during
oral and this could be a huge turn off.

The truth is that you can easily simulate deep throat
action without having to engulf his whole penis in your
mouth. Place the tip of his shaft between your lips and
grab the rest of him with your hands. Massage him by
twisting your hands in opposite directions while teasing

his head with your lips and tongue.

6. Biting anywhere down there

Though some guys can handle—or crave—a little nibble, let's just steer clear of adding teeth to any oral action unless he specifically requests otherwise. Just like women don't want teeth muddling the tongue and pressure action happening when guys go down, he doesn't want a swift bite during a blowjob.

If you feel the need to use your chompers, let your hands work his penis and nibble gently on his ear or nipples. These multiple sensations could be the spice that immediately sends him over the edge.

Just don't think that sexy reaction means he wants your teeth down there. He doesn't.

7. Not Getting It Wet Enough

If I had to guess, I'd say this problem stems from wanting to be sanitary, but like, you're just going to have to get over it. Like all sex, the messier and grosser a blow job is, the better it is. These are just the facts of life. And, I mean, think about how ridiculous it is: you're already putting a dick in your mouth, but you're going to draw the line at getting your own saliva all over you? It doesn't really make any sense. Just using your tongue with reckless abandon isn't enough. You need to get the dick wet. Spit on it. Gag on it a little so you're forced to produce more saliva (this has the added bonus of making the guy think he's swinging a third leg even if his dick is the size of a pig in a blanket). Spit on your hand and then use your hand for a bit. Are you basically imploding in on yourself out of discomfort? Too bad. But also, low-key same.

8. Not Keeping A Consistent Rhythm

The rest of the list items come courtesy of my friend Avery, a certified male. When I asked him, "What are the biggest mistakes women make when giving blow jobs?" His first answer was "Not keeping a consistent rhythm." When I asked why (because wouldn't you want to switch things up a little so nobody gets bored and I don't asphyxiate?) he said that you don't want to be constantly changing things up if you actually want the guy to finish. Like, if a guy was going down on you, would you want him changing his technique every 10 seconds? No. By all means, change things up when you get bored or your jaw starts to hurt, but don't switch techniques like an overzealous DJ at a bar switching songs.

9. Acting Like It's A Favor

This really goes for anyone, and for any sex act. First up:

You should not be doing something you do not want to and/or are not comfortable doing. End of discussion. But, as amazing as your BJ skills may be, you should not walk around like you're the Queen of England for deigning to put genitals in your mouth. (What a low bar for us as a society that would be.) I mean, how annoying would it be if every time a guy went down on you, he basically guilted you into doing something in return for him? Oh, what's that? Guys already do that when they buy you a drink, take you out, or cat-call you on the street? Right, but like, how much do we hate when they do that? Exactly. Do it because you want to, and because you forgot to buy him a birthday present, but don't do it in order to force him to shower you with endless praise and thanks.

10. A limp grip

Since women don't have their own parts to tug on, it's hard to imagine the line between a fair squeeze and a cobra strangle. But a top mistake women make during oral sex is that the grip isn't tight enough to cause that titillating friction.

To be sure you're gripping it right, grip your hand around his shaft and ask him to put his hand around yours. Have him show you a squeeze that's comfortable to him and learn from his wise teaching. All guys are different, so trust his answer! And if he doesn't tell you what feels good for his body, it's really his loss.

11. Making it a standard precursor to sex

The easiest way to turn your routine into a rut is to turn every blowie into a sex session. If he knows what to expect every single time, it won't be nearly as satisfying for either of you.

Pick a random night out to whisper in his ear, "You're

getting the best blowjob of your life later. Can't wait to get home!" When you and your hard-all-night guy get ready for action, let him know that you aren't stopping until he's finished.

CHAPTER 6

THINGS HE WANTS YOU TO KNOW ABOUT

ORAL SEX

As someone who writes about sex for a living, I'm asked about blow jobs all the time. Every mouth is different, every penis is different, every man and woman is different. So it shouldn't surprise anyone that each and every blow job is going to be a different, specific experience too. I can't speak for every guy, but odds are most guys definitely want you to know several things on this list.

The most important thing to remember? If you're giving him a blow job in the first place, that's half the battle. He's already enjoying himself. Here's what else he wants you to know:

1. He just wants you to relax.

Seriously. It's a blow job. He's just happy you're here and doing things with his penis. Don't get in your own head about it. I know that's basically what a football coach would say, but playing football and going down have a lot in common. For one, I hear they're both exhausting.

2. Closing his eyes doesn't mean he's falling asleep.

He's enjoying himself. He'll likely alternate between watching you with a giant smile on his face and closing his eyes to enjoy what's happening. Blow jobs are passive for him, and that's part of the appeal if we're being honest; he doesn't have to do anything. He doesn't even need to keep his eyes open if he doesn't want to.

3. He's going to give you as much warning as he can before he orgasms.

But it still might not be enough. Please don't be mad at him though. Sometimes it sneaks up on him and he's screaming, "I'm going to come!" with urgency because he wants you to have all the time he can possibly give you to prepare, not because he thinks it's funny to spring it on you like this is a horrible.

4. He's putting a lot of faith in you, so please be careful with your teeth.

This is an exercise in trust. It is a very vulnerable time for a man and his junk. Basically, it's a trust fall for his penis.

5. When it's time for liftoff.

please do not point his penis up at his face or into a dark corner of the room. No one wants to get cum all over themselves or find a bunch of it encrusted on their couch when they're cleaning their room a month later. I mean, a day later. All men clean their room daily.

6. Being told our semen tastes terrible makes us feel bad.

That semen was prepared with love, just for you. I'm not saying you need to savor each note like a fine wine, but if you hate it, just be polite about it.

7. If you don't want to give one, he doesn't want you to either.

If you don't like giving blow jobs, don't offer them up. It's as simple as that. If you think he takes too long, or your jaw cramps up, or you just don't like it, don't put yourself through it. Nobody has fun when one partner is clearly not enjoying themselves. Do other sex stuff instead.

8. Don't be offended if he doesn't want to kiss right after.

Some guys don't love the idea of kissing you with the fresh taste of their own semen on your breath. It's nothing personal, and he is still very grateful. Hey, you might not love it when he kisses you right after he goes down on you either. If it's really bothering you, though, don't be afraid to talk to him about it.

9. You shouldn't stress spitting or swallowing.

Let it be said: No serious relationship ever collapses because of a reticence to treat his ejaculate like a four-course meal. Don't sweat it.

10. He knows he needs to return the favor.

Believe me when I say he's going to want to Pay it except without the part at the end where he gets stabbed. If he doesn't, this is the kind of shit you need to call him out on. He might be oblivious, he might be in an orgasm-induced sex coma, but either way, refusing to reciprocate is not OK, and you damn well should tell him so.

11. Keep in mind that if you blow him to completion, you're not having sex right away.

Don't back yourself into a corner here. If you're hoping to get busy with straight-up P-in-V sex after all your efforts, it's going to be tough for him to do that after he just came.

12. Enthusiasm goes a long way.

It's true for most things in life, and it's true for blow jays.

Conclusion

When a man receives a blowjob, he's generally extremely grateful. If a woman swallows his semen, he looks at it as a huge honor. Don't ask me why because no man could really explain it. If you can learn to truly enjoy the whole process, you'll have an unbelievably happy man on your hands. We strongly believe that this book will be of great help to you in honing your blowjob skills.

OTHER BOOKS BY THE AUTHOR

1. HOW TO TEASE, PLEASE AND GIVE HIM GREATEST SEX EVER: SUPER HOT LOVE MAKING TECHNIQUES TO PLEASURE AND SATISFY YOUR MAN IN BED SEXUALLY

2. ORAL SEX GUIDEBOOK FOR MEN: HOW TO EAT HER OUT AND GIVE HER BIG-O EVERY TIME

3. HOW TO GIVE HIM AN INCREDIBLE HANDJOB: IN DEPTH HANDJOB TIPS THAT WILL CAUSE HIM TO ERUPT IN BED

4. TALKING DIRTY TO YOUR MAN: SEXTINGS, PHONE TALKS AND WHAT TO SAY DURING SEX THAT WILL TURN HIM ON, PLEASE, TEASE AND DRIVE HIM CRAZY

5. HOW TO PLEASURE AND SATISFY YOUR MAN IN BED SEXUALLY: HOTTEST SEX TIPS EVERY WOMAN SHOULD FOLLOW

6. TALKING DIRTY TO YOUR WOMAN: SWEET SEXY THINGS YOU CAN SAY TO HER TO MAKE HER HORNY AND WET INSTANTLY

7. HOW TO GIVE HIM THE PERFECT BLOWJOB THAT WILL BLOW HIM AWAY: ORAL SEX IDEAS, TIPS, SKILLS, TECHNIQUES AND POSITIONS TO HELP YOU GIVE YOUR MAN

A MIND BLOWING, TOE-CURLING, ORGASMIC BJ

8. CUNNILINGUS (ORAL SEX) GUIDE TO GIVING HER MULTIPLE ORGASMS: MEN'S GUIDE TO GIVING HER GOOD HEAD THAT WILL MAKE HER SCREAM, MOAN, SHAKE, QUAKE AND SQUIRT

9. SUPER BLOWJOB TIPS, SECRETS, IDEAS, TECHNIQUES AND POSITIONS: HOW TO USE THEM TO TURN HIM ON, RIDE, TEASE, PLEASE, PLEASURE, SATISFY AND DRIVE YOUR MAN CRAZY IN BED (ORAL SEX GUIDEBOOK FOR WOMEN)

ALL AVAILABLE ON AMAZON AS E-BOOKS AND PAPERBACKS

Made in United States
North Haven, CT
15 July 2023

38976065R00059